PEN & BRUSH
LETTERING
& ALPHABETS

PEN & BRUSH LETTERING & ALPHABETS

ENLARGED SIXTEENTH EDITION

EDITED BY
STUART BOOTH &
JOHN DOUET

BLANDFORD PRESS
POOLE · NEW YORK · SYDNEY

Blandford Press
an imprint of
Cassell plc
Artillery House, Artillery Row
London SW1P 1RT

First published 1929
Fourteenth edition 1967
Fifteenth edition 1970
Reprinted six times
Sixteenth edition 1986
Reprinted 1987, 1988

British Library Cataloguing in Publication Data

Pen and brush lettering and alphabets—
  16th ed.
  1. Lettering   2. Calligraphy
  I. Booth, Stuart   II. Douet, John
  745.6'1   NK3600

ISBN 0 7137 1932 X

Distributed in the United States by
Sterling Publishing Co. Inc,
2 Park Avenue, New York, N.Y. 10016

Distributed in Australia by
Capricorn Link (Australia) Pty Ltd.
PO Box 665, Lane Cove, NSW 2066

Printed in Great Britain at the Bath Press, Avon

CONTENTS

INTRODUCTION

THE lettering which we use to-day has been handed down from early times. In fact it has been used for more than two thousand years, for our present main upright alphabet, whatever variety of "face" it may have, was derived from the Romans and is known as "Roman." We may distort this lettering, we may vary it, we may modernize it or do what we will, but always we come back with a sigh of relief to the pure Roman. It has a serenity, repose, a simplicity and above all a clarity which make it one of the greatest symbols of civilization. The small letters or miniscules, in printer's terms "lower case," have been evolved with the demand for flowing speed and there is no classic reference such as the Trajan inscription as in the upper case.

The following pages contain a selection of alphabets which act as a reference to the student, designer, or the professional sign and showcard writer and commercial artist. It is because of the variety of lettering which is in use to-day that there is need for such a book as this, which has now gone into fifteen impressions and has become a standard reference book.

In modern practice, lettering has become part of a power of publicity and propaganda. So much depends on lettering to convey the meaning, the emotion, or even the atmosphere, that it has become a work which at all times calls for thought, skill, and originality.

Lettering is like the voice of the elocutionist. It can portray joy and melancholia, it can shout or whisper, it can be loud and blatant or soft and refined, it can strike a note of urgency or of restraint; and these are the qualities which the modern advertiser and user of lettering wishes to employ. The alphabets shown are designed for use on a great variety of occasions. How and when is, of course, at the discretion of the letterer. The Roman carries dignity, the heavy grotesque letter clamours for attention, script may denote urgency. Each alphabet expresses something different.

It is necessary to mention that numerous types of lettering on one design or card cause confusion and decrease legibility and are consequently to be avoided. It is best that styles should be related, using for example upper case for headlines and lower case for body matter, and perhaps italics or script for something which should be outstanding. It is interesting to see how a firm can build up its own individuality in advertising by always using the same type of lettering. An advertiser is often recognized by the style of lettering in his announcements before the name is glanced at.

The alphabets in this book have been divided broadly into sections:—The Serif, Italics, Sans Serif, Shadow, Script, Numerals, Unusual Styles. Where samples of type are shown, these have mostly been selected from the "MONOTYPE" range.

It is impossible to cover every particular type of lettering that has existed or does exist, but basic alphabets in general use to-day are included, and numerous examples of how they can be adapted. From these the artist will find sufficient material to exercise his creative imagination.

ABCDEFGI HJKLMNO PQRSTUV WXYZ

PERPETUA LIGHT TITLING which has the matchless proportions of the classical Roman letter.

abcdefghij klmnopqr stuvwxyz

PERPETUA—Roman lower case.

ABCDEFGH
IJKLMNOP
QRSTUVW
XYZ

abcdefghijklm
nopqrstuvwxyz

BODONI—A much used modern style Roman in which strength is combined with delicacy because of the contrasting heavy descenders and fine ascenders.

ABCDEFGH
IJKLMNOP
QRSTUVW
XYZ

abcdefghijk
lmnopqrstu
vwxyz

ULTRA BODONI—This striking, heavy letter gives an
effect of weight and boldness.

ABCDEFGHIJ KLMNOPQR STUVWXYZ

abcdefghij klmnopqr stuvwxyz

BEMBO—One of the loveliest of all old-face designs.

ABCDEFGH
IJKLMNO
PQRSTUV
WXYZ

abcdefgh
ijklmnopq
rstuvwxyz

TIMES BOLD—A twentieth-century contribution to type design.

ABCDEFGHIJ

KLMNOPQRS

TUVWXYZ

abcdefghij

klmnopqrs

tuvwxyz

SLIM BLACK—A condensed letter of distinction.

ABCDEFGHJ
KLMNOPQR
STUVWXYZ

abcdefghijkln
mopqrstuw
vxyz

MONARCH—A pen-lettered alphabet combining strength with dignity.
Its characteristic serifs can best be put in finally with the brush.

A B C D E F G H I J
K L M N O P Q R
S T U V W X Y Z

a b c d e f g h i j k l m
n o p q r s t u v w x y z

ROCKWELL—An even thickness letter with slab serifs.

ABCDEFGHIJ KLMNOPQR STVUWXYZ

abcdefghijklm nopqrstuvwxyz

PERPETUA—The italic form of the alphabet on page 7.   Note the slight modification in the proportion of letters and the elliptical curves.

ABCDE

FGHIJK

LMNOP

QRSTU

VWXYZ

A single-stroke broad-nib alphabet of classical proportions. A good example
of fine penmanship of a style used in formal work.

a b c d e f

g h i j k l

m n o p q

r s t u v

w x y z

ABCDEFGH
IJKLMNOP
QRSTUVW
XYZ

abcdefghijklmn
opqrstuvwxyz

GILL BOLD SANS SERIF ITALIC

A B C D E F G

H I J K L M N

O P Q R S T U

V W X Y Z

abcdefghij
klmnopqr
stuvwxyz

TIMES BOLD ITALIC—the italic version of the alphabet shown on page 11.

ABCDEFGHIJ KLMNOPQRS TUVWXYZ&

abcdefghijklmno pqrstuvwxyz

1234567890

GOUDY BOLD ITALIC—An attractive, legible letter, which has more strength than most of the italic faces.

ABCDEFG
HIJKLMN
OPQRSTU
VWXYZ

abcdefghijklm
nopqrstuvwxyz
1234567890

A single-stroke pen alphabet. This is particularly suitable for rapid show-card and price ticket work, as its very essence is simplicity. For this page a Myers No. 1 broad nib was used.

ABCDEFG
HIJKLMN
OPQRSTU
VWXYZ

abcdefghi
jklmnopqr
stuvwxyz

1234567890

A slightly expanded italic sans-serif letter, based on FTF's 'Washington' design, which is becoming increasingly popular. For best effect it should be used sparingly, and with plenty of white space.

ABCDEF
GHIJKL
MNOPQ
RSTUVW
XYZ

abcdefghijklmn
opqrstuvwxyz

GILL SANS TITLING—A legible, pleasant and very readable face. Suitable for headings where copy is short, but if used to any great extent the effect is monotonous. Gill Sans lower case is shown in the frame.

A B C D E
F G H I J K
L M N O P
Q R S T U
V W X Y Z

GILL SANS BOLD TITLING—gives weight.

ABCDEFG
HIJKLMN
OPQRSTU
VWXYZ

abcdefghij
klmnopqr
stuvwxyz

GILL SANS EXTRA BOLD gives emphasis and strength.

ABCDEFGHIJKL
MNOPQRSTU
VWXYZ&

abcdefghijklmn
opqrstuvwxyz

1234567890

FUTURA LIGHT—A notable contribution to the sans-serif series
and which is especially useful where delicacy of effect is desired.

ABCDEFG HIJKLMN OPQRST UVWXYZ

abcdefghijklmn opqrstuvwxyz

ALBERTUS has a distinct character of its own and in its conformation
it is not unlike Gill.

ABCDEFGHIJK

LMNOPQRST

UVWXYZ&

GOTHIC CONDENSED—A letter of a very striking design in the sans-serif class. As with all condensed types, this can be used where economy of space is necessary.

abcdefghijkl
mnopqrstuv
wxyz

1234567890

ABCDEFG
HIJKLMN
OPQRSTU
VWXYZ

ELONGATED ROMAN SHADED

ABCDEFG
HIJKLMN
OPQRSTU
VWXYZ

SANS SERIF SHADED—An elongated style with legibility and
distinction.

31

ABCDE
FGHIJK
LMNOPV
QRSTU
WXYZ
1234567
890

GILL SHADOW—The shadow effect here gives a sense of considerable depth.

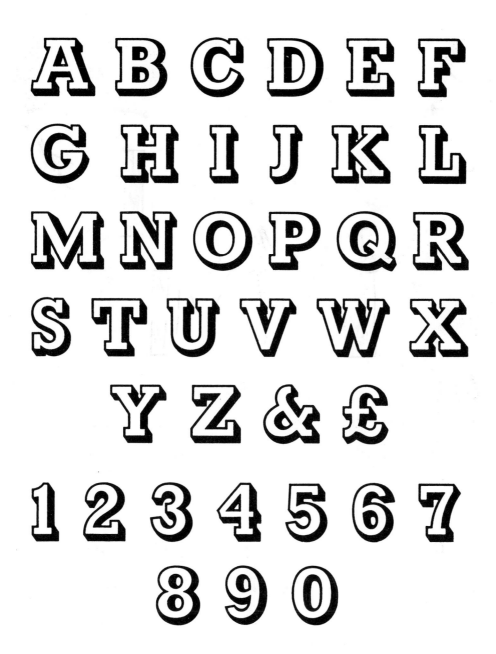

ROCKWELL SHADOW—A sturdy letter that looks effective in either one or two colours.

A B C D E
F G H I J
K L M N
O P Q R
S T U V
W X Y Z

A Roman letter with an unusual shading effect.

A B C D E F G

H I J K L M N

O P Q R S T U

V W X Y Z &

abcdefghijklmnopqrstu

vwxyz

1234567890

BERNHARD CURSIVE BOLD—There is much grace in the form of
this modern script.

A B C D E
F G H I J
K L M N O
P Q R S T
U V V W
W X Y Z

abcdefghijklmn
oppqrrstuvwxy

PEN SCRIPT, as this style is known, is one of the oldest forms
of script and remains in everyday use.

ABCDEFG
HIJKLMN
OPQRSTU
VWXYZ

abcdefghijklm
nopqrstuvwxyz

TRAFTON—A one-stroke letter dependent for its beauty on the even flow of the letters. A valuable time-saver and favourite for hand-written price tickets and showcards.

ABCDEFG
HIJKLMN
OPQRSTUV
WXYZ&

abcd
efghi
jklm

nopq
rstuv
wxyz

INFORMAL SCRIPT—Should be used sparingly as captions and not as straight copy. The light face is suitable for advertising cosmetics and the like. Where ruggedness is required it can be drawn in a bold face using a large pen.

A B C D E
F G H I J K
L M N O P
Q R S T U
V W X Y Z

This elegant yet legible style can be utilized for initials in many styles of lettering, both upright and sloping, and for the body matter in illuminated addresses, testimonials, etc.

ABCDEFG
HIJKLMN
OPQRSTU
VWXYZ

abcdefghi
jklmnopqr
stuvwxyz

An alphabet resembling 'Signal'. Heavy condensed scripts produce here and there areas of inarticulate darkness which reduce legibility. These have to be eliminated by tricks, slight falsities to the true rhythm to the style.

New Season's Displays *The Scotchman*

—Fastest Time Ever!

Old French Porcelain

A New Airline...

Yachting Club

Express When a jazz man's blue...

New World Exhibitions

Good Food News The largest range

A new Overseas Journal

United States Lines

Script lettering can speak with a variety of intonation—sometimes elegant,
or exciting; perhaps regal or racy.

Masculine

Script for Style

Parchment

Sophisticated

Ball-pointed

PEN APPLICATION

Moist Feminine

or dry

or both

Texture

Very Informal

Textile

Calligraphy

BRUSH APPLICATION

the DEGREE of and the Quality of exaggeration Possible in Advertising script is determined by the structure

Varieties of script showing its endless possibilities.

of the letters —
especially letters
of the first
and by the Message or
AND
and by the words
of the WORD
that (must) be
written

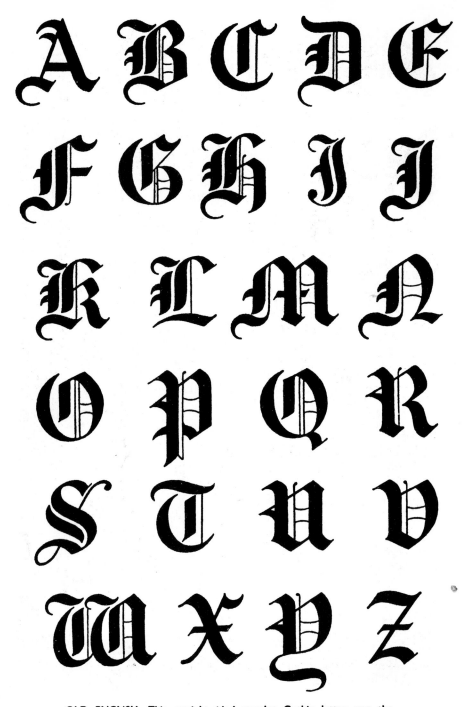

OLD ENGLISH—This straight-sided angular Gothic letter was the original style used for the printed page. There are, of course, many different interpretations in present-day use, but the basic forms remain the same. Hair lines for embellishment should be avoided since they detract from legibility.

OLD ENGLISH LOWER CASE

1 2 3
4 5 6 7 8 9 0

CONDENSED SANS SERIF

---

1 2 3
4 5 6 7 8 9 0

GILL SANS BOLD CONDENSED

TRAFTON

1 2 3
4 5 6 7 8 9 0

Free and easy style for
script lettering

1 2 3
4 5 6 7 8 9 0

PERPETUA

1 2 3
4 5 6 7 8 9 0

GILL SANS MEDIUM ITALIC

ABCDEFGHIJKLM
NOPQRSTUVWXYZ

CENTURY

abcdefghijklm
nopqrstuvwxyz

1234567890

PLAYBILL—This dates from the days of the theatre poster and makes a heavy impact with its slab-like serifs and the emphasis on the horizontal strokes, which is in contrast to almost every other letter-form. Still surprisingly popular, it is an effective display face.

A B C D E F G

H I J K L M N

O P Q R S T U

V W X Y Z

a b c d e f g h

i j k l m n o p q

r s t u v w x y z

1 2 3 4 5 6 7 8 9

STUDIO—Based on the Amsterdam Type Foundry's design, this is a modern one-stroke alphabet, especially suitable for showcard work.

ABCDEFGHIJ KLMNOPQRS TUVWXYZ&

abcdefghijklm nopqrstuvwxyz

1234567890

METROPOLIS—A modern heavy letter, almost in the spirit of Ultra
Bodoni, but free in its style.

A B C D E F G
H I J K L M N
O P Q R S T U
V W X Y Z

a b c d e f g h i j k
l m n o p q r s t u v
w x y z

1 2 3 4 5 6 7 8 9 0

An italic slab-serif letter, based on Ludlow Karnak heavy italic (by courtesy of Odhams Press). This style of heavy squat letter is much favoured for exhibition signs and shop fascia board work.

ABCDE
FGHIJK
LMNOP
QRSTU
VWXYZ

STENCIL based on the actual form of letters stencilled on packing
cases—gives a note of the unusual.

ABCDEFGHI
JKLMNOPQR
STUVWXY & Z

abcdefghijklm
nopqrs_tuvwx
y and 3 /

MODERN THICK AND THIN—The letter height is twice
as thick as the average width.

ABCDEF
GHIJKLN
MOPQRS
TUVWXY
Z &
123456789

Adapted from the well-known printer's type 'Cooper Black.' A speedy
bold alphabet for poster and showcard work.

abcdefgh
ijklmnop
qrstuvwx
yz

The lower case of the alphabet opposite. The style combines maximum
boldness with clear-cut lines and complete legibility.

ABCDEF
GHIJKL
MNOPQ
RSTUV
WXYZ

Another modern thick and thin sans-serif, which is extremely well designed, derived from Crous Vidal's 'Paris' typeface. This italic version has many possible variations and weight.

A B C D E F
G H I J K L
M N O P Q
R S T U V W
X Y Z abcdefghijk
lmnopqrstuvwxyz !_?

MODERN FRENCH for work requiring a light letter of simplicity
and a touch of exclusiveness.

ABCDEFGHIJ
KLMNOPQRS
TUVWXYZ

abcdefghijklm
nopqrstuvwxyz

1234567890

An example of a brush script lettering based on ATF's 'Dom Casual',
designed by Peter Dom.

ABCDEF
GHIJKLM
NOPQRST
UVWXYZ

abcdefghij
klmnopqrst
uvwxyz&!?

EASTERN—An alphabet designed on Oriental characters, principally the wedge in the crescent. There are obvious occasions for its use and it is quickly written.

ABCDE
FGHIJK
LMNOP
QRSTU
VWXYZ

CHRISTMAS—An example of how a season atmosphere can be
introduced into the letter.

PEN-WRITTEN CAPITALS — From *The Pen's Transcendency*, a Writing Book by E. Cocker, 1660. Cocker was so emphatically *the* English writing-master of his day as to have given rise to the phrase, "According to Cocker."

MODERN GOTHIC CAPITALS — Fanciful, but no violence to accepted form.
An alphabet in which it is permitted even to hide the meaning so long as it is
still there.

EFGH

NOPQ

WXYZ

ABCDEFG
HIJKLMN
OPQRSTU
VWXYZ&

abcdefghijk
lmnopqrstu
vwxyz& ·§·
1234567890

PEN-WRITTEN ALPHABETS AND NUMERALS — Percy J. Smith.

abcde efghi klmn opqrs stuvx

STONE LETTERING — From inscriptions at Osnabrück, Germany. Halting
between majuscule and miniscule forms. 1742-56

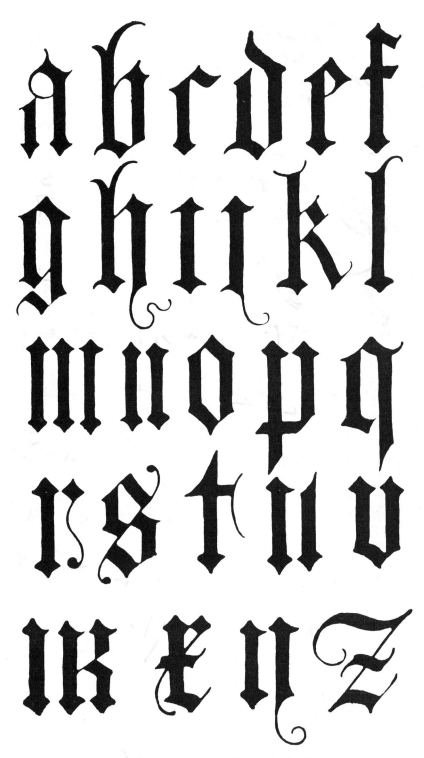

ALBRECHT DÜRER GERMAN MINISCULE — Early 16th century.

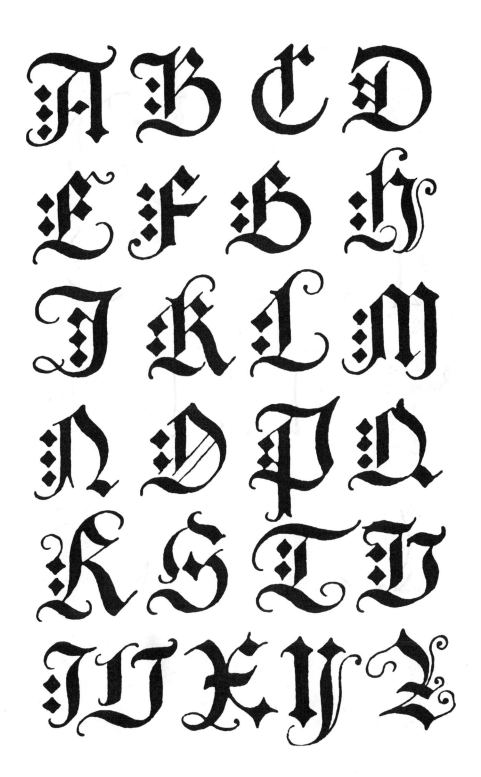

ALBRECHT DÜRER GOTHIC CAPITALS — Penwork. Early 16th century.

ABCDE FGHIJK LMNOP QRSTU VWXYZ

abcdefghijklmn opqrstuvwxyz

STENCILLED ALPHABET — adapted from E. Grasset and M. P. Verneuil.

NOTES

NOTES

8534